Foreign Currency Accounting

Steven M. Bragg

AccountingTools®

Published by AccountingTools, Inc., Centennial, Colorado.

ISBN 978-1-64221-288-4

For more information about AccountingTools® products, visit our Web site at www.accountingtools.com.

Table of Contents

About the Author

Steven Bragg, CPA, has been the chief financial officer or controller of four companies, as well as a consulting manager at Ernst & Young. He received a master's degree in finance from Bentley College, an MBA from Babson College, and a Bachelor's degree in Economics from the University of Maine. He has been a two-time president of the Colorado Mountain Club, and is an avid alpine skier, mountain biker, and certified master diver. Mr. Bragg resides in Centennial, Colorado. He has written more than 300 books and courses, including *New Controller Guidebook*, *GAAP Guidebook*, and *Payroll Management*.

Steven maintains the accountingtools.com web site, which contains continuing professional education courses, the Accounting Best Practices podcast, and thousands of articles on accounting subjects.

Chapter 1
Financial Statement Translation

Introduction

Foreign currency accounting covers three main topics, which are:

- The translation of financial statements
- Foreign currency transactions
- Foreign currency hedging

In this chapter, we address the first topic, and then move on to the transaction and hedging issues in the second chapter. A third chapter addresses several ancillary issues, including internal audit tasks and foreign currency disclosures.

When a business has subsidiaries in foreign countries, they may deal largely in the local currency, and so have chosen to produce financial statements that are denominated in the local currency. If so, the parent entity needs to convert these financial statements into the denomination of its reporting currency before completing a consolidation of all subsidiary financial statements into its own financials, using a single currency. In the following sections, we address the steps required to translate the financial statements of subsidiaries into the currency of the parent entity, and note how this impacts the period-end closing process.

> **Note:** The following discussion assumes that the reporting currency of an organization is the U.S. dollar. This does not have to be the case. For example, it is possible for a business to report using its local currency, while still being in conformity with generally accepted accounting principles.

A Note Regarding Consolidations and the Equity Method

In the following sections of this chapter, we will refer to consolidations and the equity method. A financial statement *consolidation* is intended to present the results and financial position of a parent entity and its subsidiaries, as though they were a single entity. It is also possible to have consolidated financial statements for a portion of a group of companies, such as for a subsidiary and those other entities owned by the subsidiary. Consolidated financial statements are useful for reviewing the financial position and results of an entire group of commonly-owned businesses. Otherwise, reviewing the results of individual businesses within the group does not give an indication of the financial health of the group as a whole.

A consolidation is typically conducted when the parent entity has a controlling financial interest in other entities. A controlling financial interest is considered to be present when there is a direct or indirect majority voting interest of more than 50% of the outstanding voting shares.

When a company owns an interest in another business that it does not control (such as a corporate joint venture), it may use the *equity method* to account for its ownership interest. The equity method is designed to measure changes in the economic results of the investee, by requiring the investor to recognize its share of the profits or losses recorded by the investee.

The key determining factor in the use of the equity method is having significant influence over the operating and financial decisions of the investee. The primary determinant of this level of control is owning at least 20% of the voting shares of the investee, though this measurement can be repudiated by evidence that the investee opposes the influence of the investor. Other types of evidence of significant influence are controlling a seat on the board of directors, active participation in the decisions of the investee, or swapping management personnel with the investee.

In those cases in which a business has an interest in a foreign entity, its use of either a consolidation or the equity method will require the foreign currency accounting described in the following sections.

Financial Statement Translation

A company may have subsidiaries located in other countries, and creates financial statements for those subsidiaries that are denominated in the local currency. If so, the parent company will need to translate the results of these subsidiaries into the currency used by the parent company when it creates consolidated financial statements for the entire entity (called the *reporting currency*). The steps in this process are as follows:

1. Determine the functional currency of the foreign entity.
2. Remeasure the financial statements of the foreign entity into the reporting currency of the parent company.
3. Record gains and losses on the translation of currencies.

The concept of the functional currency is somewhat different when there is a highly inflationary economy. This difference is noted later in the Hyperinflationary Effects subsection.

Determination of Functional Currency

The financial results and financial position of a company should be measured using its functional currency, which is the currency that the company uses in the majority of its business transactions.

If a foreign business entity operates primarily within one country and is not dependent upon the parent company, its functional currency is the currency of the country in which its operations are located. However, there are other foreign operations that are more closely tied to the operations of the parent company, and whose financing is mostly supplied by the parent or other sources that use the dollar. In this latter case, the functional currency of the foreign operation is probably the dollar. These two examples anchor the ends of a continuum on which foreign operations will be found. Unless an operation is clearly associated with one of the two examples provided, it is likely that it will be necessary to make a determination of functional currency based on the unique circumstances pertaining to each entity. For example, the functional currency may be difficult to determine if a business conducts an equal amount of business in two different countries. An examination of the factors noted in the following exhibit can assist in determining a functional currency.

Determination of Functional Currency

Indicators	Indicates Use of Foreign Currency as Functional Currency	Indicates use of Reporting Currency as Functional Currency
Cash flow	The cash flows relating to an entity's assets and liabilities are primarily in the foreign currency, and have no direct impact on the cash flows of the parent	The cash flows relating to an entity's assets and liabilities directly affect the cash flows of the parent and are available for remittance to it
Expenses	The labor, material, and other costs of the entity are primarily obtained locally, even though some items may be obtained via imports	The labor, material, and other costs of the entity are primarily obtained from the parent's country
Financing	Any financing obtained is primarily denominated in a foreign currency, and locally-generated funds should be able to service the entity's existing and expected debts	Financing is obtained from the parent or is in dollar-denominated obligations, or locally-generated funds are not sufficient for the servicing of existing and expected debts without a cash infusion from the parent
Intra-entity transactions	There are few intra-entity transactions, and operations are not tightly integrated with those of the parent, though there may be reliance on the competitive advantages of the parent	There are many intra-entity transactions, and operations are more likely to be tightly integrated with those of the parent; this also applies when the foreign entity is a shell corporation that holds the assets of the parent
Sales market	There is an active local market for the products of the entity, even though the entity may have significant export activity, as well	The primary market for the entity's products is the country of the parent, or sales are denominated in the currency of the parent's country
Sales price	Sales prices are mostly based on local competition and government regulations, rather than on exchange rate changes	Sales prices are mostly based on exchange rate changes, which can be driven by international price competition

Several additional factors to consider when determining the functional currency are as follows:

- *Entity with several operations*. It is possible that a foreign entity has several distinct and separable operations, each of which has different operating characteristics. Thus, one operation might be classified as using the local currency, while another operation might be designated as using the reporting currency. If so, each operation could be considered a separate entity with a different functional currency.
- *Multiple entities*. A parent entity may have a large number of divisions or branches. If so, it will be necessary to treat each one as a separate entity for the purpose of determining functional currencies.
- *Equity method investees*. When a business accounts for an investment in another entity using the equity method, this implies that the business exercises significant influence over the investee. This implied level of control could indicate that the functional currency is the reporting currency.
- *Use of multiple currencies*. There may be situations in which an operation uses multiple currencies, in which case the functional currency is not clearly identifiable. If so, management must examine the economic facts and circumstances to establish a functional currency in which the greatest degree of relevance and reliability can be achieved. When a decision is reached, document the reasons for it, in case the auditors make an inquiry.

Note: If a company is rolling out a number of essentially identical subsidiaries (such as retail stores) in a country, the operating characteristics of each entity in the group should essentially match those of the other entities. This means that it should be possible to determine the functional currency just once, and apply the same designation to every similar entity in the country.

The functional currency in which a business reports its financial results should rarely change. A shift to a different functional currency should be used only when there is a significant change in the economic facts and circumstances. If there is a change in functional currency, do not restate previously-issued financial statements into the new currency.

EXAMPLE

Armadillo Industries has a subsidiary in Australia, to which it ships its body armor products for sale to local police forces. The Australian subsidiary sells these products and then remits payments back to corporate headquarters. Armadillo should consider U.S. dollars to be the functional currency of this subsidiary.

Armadillo also owns a subsidiary in Russia, which manufactures its own body armor for local consumption, accumulates cash reserves, and borrows funds locally. This subsidiary rarely remits funds back to the parent company. In this case, the functional currency should be the Russian ruble.

Translation into Functional Currency

When the determination is made regarding what the functional currency of an entity should be, it may be found that the entity is not actually recording transactions in that currency. If so, its transactions must be remeasured into the functional currency; this must take place *before* the financial statements of the entity are translated into the reporting currency. The intent of this translation is to create the same financial statements that would have been produced if the accounting records of the entity had originally been kept in the functional currency. To create such financial statements, it will be necessary to do the following:

- Use historical exchange rates between the functional currency and the currency in which the transactions were actually recorded for the following accounts:

    o Marketable securities recorded at cost (includes equity securities and debt securities not being held to maturity)
    o Inventories recorded at cost
    o Prepaid expenses
    o Fixed assets and the associated accumulated depreciation
    o Intangible assets (such as patents, trademarks, and licenses)
    o Goodwill
    o Deferred charges
    o Deferred income
    o Common stock
    o Preferred stock
    o Revenues and expenses associated with nonmonetary items (such as the cost of goods sold, depreciation, and amortization)

- Use the current exchange rate between the functional currency and the currency in which the transactions were actually recorded for all other accounts.
- Recognize in income all exchange gains and losses caused by the remeasurement of monetary assets and liabilities that were not denominated in the functional currency.

Over the long term, the simplest way to ensure that transactions are stated in the functional currency is to initially record them in the accounting system as such; this may call for the conversion of the accounting system to a new one as of a convenient date, such as the first day of the next fiscal year. Doing so results in a complete set of fiscal year financial statements that are already in the designated functional currency.

Translation of Financial Statements

When translating the financial statements of an entity for consolidation purposes into the reporting currency of a business, translate the financial statements using the following rules:

- *Assets and liabilities.* Translate using the current exchange rate at the balance sheet date for assets and liabilities.
- *Income statement items.* Translate revenues, expenses, gains, and losses using the exchange rate as of the dates when those items were originally recognized. To reduce the associated workload, average exchange rates can be employed. See the later Use of Average Exchange Rates sub-section for more information.
- *Allocations.* Translate all cost and revenue allocations using the exchange rates in effect when those allocations are recorded. Examples of allocations are depreciation and the amortization of deferred revenues.
- *Different balance sheet date.* If the foreign entity being consolidated has a different balance sheet date than that of the reporting entity, use the exchange rate in effect as of the foreign entity's balance sheet date.
- *Profit eliminations.* If there are intra-entity profits to be eliminated as part of the consolidation, apply the exchange rate in effect on the dates when the underlying transactions took place. Average exchange rates or other approximations can be used.

If the process of converting the financial statements of a foreign entity into the reporting currency of the parent company results in a translation adjustment, report the related profit or loss in other comprehensive income (see the next sub-section).

EXAMPLE

A subsidiary of Armadillo Industries is located in Argentina, and its functional currency is the Argentine peso. The relevant peso exchange rates are:

- 0.20 to the dollar at the beginning of the year
- 0.24 to the dollar at the end of the year
- 0.22 to the dollar for the full-year weighted average rate

Financial Statement Translation

The subsidiary had no retained earnings at the beginning of the year. Based on this information, the financial statement conversion is as follows:

(000s)	Argentine Pesos	Exchange Rate	U.S. Dollars
Assets			
Cash	89,000	0.24	21,360
Accounts receivable	267,000	0.24	64,080
Inventory	412,000	0.24	98,880
Fixed assets, net	608,000	0.24	145,920
Total assets	1,376,000		330,240
Liabilities and Equity			
Accounts payable	320,000	0.24	76,800
Notes payable	500,000	0.24	120,000
Common stock	10,000	0.20	2,400
Additional paid-in capital	545,000	0.20	130,800
Retained earnings	1,000	(*)	220
Translation adjustments	0	--	20
Total liabilities and equity	1,376,000		330,240

* Reference from the following income statement

(000s)	Argentine Pesos	Exchange Rate	U.S. Dollars
Revenue	1,500,000	0.22	330,000
Expenses	1,499,000	0.22	329,780
Net income	1,000		220
Beginning retained earnings	0		0
Add: Net income	1,000	0.22	220
Ending retained earnings	1,000		220

Reporting in Other Comprehensive Income

Other comprehensive income (OCI) is a separate reporting block that can appear after the income statement or in an entirely separate statement. Gains and losses recorded in OCI are related to changes in the valuation of different assets and liabilities that have not yet been realized. The amount recorded in OCI accumulates in equity, in the accumulated other comprehensive income (AOCI) account.

Once the designated gains and losses are realized, these gains and losses are shifted into the main body of the income statement from AOCI. A sample statement of OCI appears in the following exhibit.

Sample Presentation of Other Comprehensive Income

Armadillo Industries
Statement of Other Comprehensive Income
For the Year Ended December 31, 20X2

Net income		$45,000
Other comprehensive income, net of tax		
Foreign currency translation adjustments		**2,000**
Unrealized holding gains arising during period		11,000
Defined benefit pension plans:		
Prior period service cost arising during period	-$4,000	
Net loss arising during period	-1,000	-5,000
Other comprehensive income		8,000
Comprehensive income, net of tax		$53,000

In the sample, we noted in bold the presence of foreign currency translation adjustments. These adjustments relate to transactions that have not yet been completed, and so are unrealized. Once the underlying transactions have been completed, the gains or losses will have been realized, and these adjustments will be shifted to the income statement.

Line items relating to foreign currency transactions that can appear in this statement are as follows:

- Foreign currency translation adjustments
- Gains and losses on intra-company foreign currency transactions where settlement is not planned in the foreseeable future
- Gains and losses on foreign currency translation adjustments that are net investment hedges in a foreign entity
- Changes in the fair value of available-for-sale debt securities that are denominated in a foreign currency

To see where AOCI is located, the following sample equity section of a balance sheet shows the line item. The AOCI line is stated separately from common stock, additional paid-in capital, and retained earnings.

EXAMPLE

Armadillo Industries reports accumulated other comprehensive income within the equity section of its balance sheet as follows:

Equity:	
Common stock	$1,000,000
Paid-in capital	850,000
Retained earnings	4,200,000
Accumulated other comprehensive income	**270,000**
Total equity	$6,320,000

Impact on the Statement of Cash Flows

In the statement of cash flows, state all foreign currency cash flows at their reporting currency equivalent using the exchange rates in effect when the cash flows occurred. A weighted average exchange rate may be used for this calculation if the result would be substantially the same as if the cash flow-specific rates had been used. In addition, report in the statement of cash flows the effect of exchange rate changes on cash balances held in foreign currencies. This reporting should be noted within the reconciliation of the change in cash and cash equivalents during the reporting period. A sample of this presentation follows, where the applicable line item is noted in bold.

Sample Reconciliation of Net Income to Net Cash Provided by Operating Activities

Net income		$1,000,000
Adjustments to reconcile net income to net cash provided by operating activities:		
Depreciation and amortization	$125,000	
Loss on sale of equipment	20,000	
Exchange gain	**-65,000**	
Provision for deferred taxes	32,000	
Increase in trade receivables	-250,000	
Decrease in inventories	125,000	
Decrease in trade payables	-50,000	
		-63,000
Net cash provided by operating activities		$937,000

Special Translation Situations

There can be situations in which a business records the historical cost of an asset, using in its books of record a currency different from its functional currency. The value of this currency may change in relation to the functional currency of the entity between the date when the asset was acquired and the balance sheet date. This disparity can give rise to asset valuation changes, as noted next.

Inventory Translation

A special situation can arise when inventory is being carried on the books of a subsidiary in a currency that is not the functional currency of the subsidiary. If so, and as noted earlier in the Translation of Financial Statements sub-section, the inventory must first be remeasured into the designated functional currency, using historical exchange rates. These historical costs are then compared with the market prices of the inventory as stated in the functional currency. This step can result in application of the lower of cost or market (LCM) rule, where an inventory write-down is required in the functional currency, even though no such write-down is called for in the books of the subsidiary (which use an alternative currency).

The reverse situation can also arise. A business might have recognized an LCM write-down in its books of record, using a currency that is not the designated functional currency. Once the currency has been converted to the functional currency, it is possible that the market price now exceeds the adjusted historical cost, in which case the LCM write-down can be reversed.

The LCM rule essentially states that a business must record the cost of inventory at whichever cost is lower – the original cost or its current market price (hence the name of the rule). More specifically, the rule mandates that the recognized cost of an inventory item should be reduced to a level that does not exceed its replacement cost as derived in an open market. This replacement cost is subject to the following two conditions:

- The recognized cost cannot be greater than the likely selling price minus costs of disposal (known as net realizable value).
- The recognized cost cannot be lower than the net realizable value minus a normal profit percentage.

This situation typically arises when inventory has deteriorated, or has become obsolete, or market prices have declined.

EXAMPLE

Monique Ponto produces high-end women's watches. The company has a subsidiary that operates in the independent republic of Ralston, located in the Caribbean. The subsidiary maintains its books of record in Ralston Pounds. However, the parent company has designated the functional currency of the subsidiary to be U.S. dollars. The exchange rate between the two currencies was 2 RP = 1 USD when the subsidiary bought a gold watch casing for 1,000 RP.

Or, as measured in the functional currency, the watch casing cost 500 USD. As of the balance sheet date of the subsidiary, the exchange rate had changed to 2.2 RP = 1 USD.

Scenario 1: The current replacement cost of the watch casing is 1,050 RP, which is higher than its original cost of 1,000 RP. However, when translated into USD at the current exchange rate of 2.2 RP to 1 USD, the current replacement cost in USD has declined to $477 from its original cost of $500. This calls for an inventory write-down of $23 in the functional currency financial statements.

Scenario 2: The current replacement cost of the watch casing is 1,200 RP, which is higher than its original cost of 1,000 RP. When translated into USD at the current exchange rate of 2.2 RP to 1 USD, the current replacement cost in USD has increased to $545 from its original cost of $500. No inventory write-down is required, since the market price now exceeds historical cost.

Other Asset Translation

The LCM adjustment just noted for inventory could also apply to other assets. As was the case with inventory, the situation should only occur when the conversion from a different currency to the functional currency results in the market price of an asset being below its cost. The reversal of a previous write-down can also occur under the same circumstances.

Noncontrolling Interests

There may be noncontrolling interests in a foreign entity, which are also known as minority interests. If so, allocate any accumulated translation adjustments attributable to the noncontrolling interests to the noncontrolling interests line item in the consolidated financial statements of the parent entity.

Use of Average Exchange Rates

We have noted that the remeasurement of financial statements may require the use of historical exchange rate information. It can be burdensome to keep track of these exchange rates and the dates on which the rates are to be applied. To reduce the work involved, GAAP allows the use of an average exchange rate, or other labor-saving methods that reasonably approximate the exchange rates that were more frequently applied. If an average exchange rate is used, derive a weighted average based on the volume of currency transactions in the period. For example, a reasonably accurate result might be achieved by developing an average rate for each month of the year, to be applied to those transactions occurring within each month. The translated amounts for each month are then aggregated for inclusion in the annual financial statements.

Tip: The derivation of average exchange rates should be carefully documented, since the auditors will need to review this information as part of their year-end audit procedures.

No Applicable Period-end Exchange Rate

There may be no foreign exchange rate available at the end of a reporting period for use in translating the financial statements. For example, foreign exchange trading may have been temporarily suspended. If so, use the first exchange rate that is available on the next date on which foreign exchange transactions can be made. The following example illustrates the point.

EXAMPLE

Icelandic Cod (despite its name) is based in the United States, and its reporting currency is the U.S. dollar. It owns a subsidiary on the tiny principality of Heard Island, which uses the Heard Dollar (HD). Icelandic Cod closes its fiscal year on December 31. The following dates and exchange rates apply to the situation:

Date	Exchange Rate	Commentary
12/30/X1	3 HD : 1 USD	Currency markets are open and operating normally
12/31/X1	--	Official devaluation of the HD is announced by the Heard government; currency trading is suspended until the devaluation has been completed
1/1/X2	--	Banks and currency exchanges are closed for the holidays
1/2/X2	4 HD : 1 USD	New exchange rate is set by the Heard government; this rate is also effective for all unsettled transactions

There was no valid market exchange rate at year-end, so the exchange rate to be used for year-end consolidation purposes is the 4:1 exchange rate established on January 2 of the following year.

Hyperinflationary Effects

An entity may find itself operating in an environment that has cumulative inflation of 100% or more. If this level of inflation continues over a three-year period, a country is considered to have a highly inflationary economy. The same outcome still applies if the cumulative inflation is less than 100%, but the trend of inflation, combined with other economic factors, suggests that the economy is highly inflationary.

EXAMPLE

The government of Mirandela, a small country located high in the Andes mountain range, has been printing money to pay for its social programs. The result is the following annual inflation rate:

	Year 1	Year 2	Year 3	Year 4	Year 5	Year 6
Annual inflation rate	4%	7%	21%	34%	42%	39%
Cumulative 3-year rate*	--	--	35%	73%	130%	164%

   * Calculated as a compounded 3-year inflation rate

Mirandela's economy for Years 5 and 6 is classified as highly inflationary, since the cumulative 3-year rate exceeds 100%. The slight decline in the inflation rate in Year 6 does not overcome the cumulative 3-year rate.

EXAMPLE

The adjacent country of Evora also suffers from a high rate of inflation, as noted in the following table. In this case, the government has been slowly reducing its expenditures, but the inflation rate continues to be high.

	Year 1	Year 2	Year 3	Year 4	Year 5	Year 6
Annual inflation rate	23%	27%	32%	24%	22%	21%
Cumulative 3-year rate*	--	--	106%	108%	100%	83%

   * Calculated as a compounded three-year inflation rate

In this case, the cumulative 3-year rate has dropped below the 100% threshold in Year 6. Nonetheless, the trend of inflation remains high, so it would be appropriate to continue to classify the economy as being highly inflationary.

EXAMPLE

The third of this group of countries is Pombal, whose government has clamped down harder on inflation, yielding the results shown in the following table:

	Year 1	Year 2	Year 3	Year 4	Year 5	Year 6
Annual inflation rate	3%	7%	49%	27%	11%	4%
Cumulative 3-year rate*	--	--	64%	102%	110%	47%

   * Calculated as a compounded three-year inflation rate

In this case, the economy should no longer be considered highly inflationary, for two reasons. First, the cumulative 3-year inflation rate has dropped sharply. And second, there is no evidence that the economy continues to be inflationary. Instead, the information in the table indicates that the country suffered from a brief inflationary spike that is now over.

When the determination is made that an economy is highly inflationary, remeasure the financial statements of the entity operating in that environment as though the functional currency were the reporting currency.

If the economy is no longer considered to be hyperinflationary, restate the financial statements of the relevant entity so that the local currency is now the functional currency. This means translating the reporting currency amounts into the local currency amounts at the current exchange rate on the date of change; these translated amounts then become the new functional currency for the nonmonetary assets and liabilities of the entity.

EXAMPLE

A subsidiary of Armadillo Industries is operating in a highly inflationary economy. On March 31 of 20X3, it bought a machine for 50,000 units of the local currency. The exchange rate at that time was five units of the local currency to one U.S. dollar, so the equivalent cost of the machine in U.S. dollars was $10,000. Five years later, on March 31, 20X8, the machine's net book value on the subsidiary's books has declined to 25,000 units of the local currency, due to ongoing depreciation. On March 31 of 20X8, hyperinflation has altered the exchange rate to 25 to one U.S. dollar. During this time, the parent company has been using the historical exchange rate to account for the machine, so the recorded amount has declined to $5,000, based on the depreciation incurred during the intervening years.

On April 1 of 20X8, Armadillo's management no longer considers the local economy of the subsidiary to be highly inflationary, so it establishes a new cost basis for the equipment by translating the current $5,000 cost of the machine back into the local currency at the current exchange rate of 25:1. This means the functional accounting basis for the machine on April 1 of 20X8 would be 125,000 units of the local currency.

Derecognition of a Foreign Entity Investment

When a company sells or liquidates its investment in a foreign entity, complete the following steps to account for the situation:

- Remove the translation adjustment recorded in equity for the investment
- Report a gain or loss in the period in which the sale or liquidation occurs

If a company only sells a portion of its investment in a foreign entity, recognize only a pro rata portion of the accumulated translation adjustment recorded in equity.

A sale or liquidation is considered to have occurred when a controlling financial interest in the foreign entity has been lost.

Impact of Financial Statement Translation on Closing the Books

The preceding discussion of financial statement translation is a key part of the process that a business undergoes to close the books at the end of a reporting period. The translation process requires high-level analysis of the functional currency at long intervals, as well as a detailed translation into (sometimes) the functional currency and (always) the reporting currency. The following bullet points illustrate the need for additional closing steps:

- *Functional currency designation*. The functional currency will likely only need to be set once, after which it should be sufficient to occasionally revisit the original arguments for the functional currency designation, and see if they have changed. Consequently, we suggest the following additions to the closing checklist:
  - *New subsidiaries*. See if any new subsidiaries were acquired during the reporting period. If so, designate the functional currency of each of these entities. Consult with the auditors to see if they are in agreement regarding the designation. [every closing period]
  - *Review status*. Examine the documentation supporting the current designation of functional currency for each foreign entity, and adjust as necessary. This could be part of the annual audit, in the form of a discussion with the auditors. [beginning of each fiscal year]

- *Translate into functional currency*. In the rare cases where it is needed, the translation of financial statements into the functional currency of an entity could be time-consuming, and so could delay the closing process. To mitigate this issue, prepare a standard spreadsheet-based conversion template, and create a system for compiling average exchange rates that can be reliably prepared and then plugged into the template. [every closing period]

- *Translate into reporting currency*. A translation of the financial statements of an entity from its functional currency into the reporting currency will also be needed, and will be prepared close to the end of the closing process. To keep this translation from delaying the close to an excessive extent, have a conversion template prepared into which the trial balance of an entity can be entered, and from which a reporting currency trial balance can be extracted. Create a well-documented exchange rate averaging process whose results can be easily plugged into the conversion template. [every closing period]

- *Recognize LCM changes*. There may be rare cases in which the lower of cost or market rule will result in a write-down or write-up of the inventory valuation. This requires a detailed investigation at the local level only after the functional currency conversion has taken place. The examination will undoubtedly introduce a delay into the closing process, and so should be completed quite infrequently. [end of fiscal year]

There are two best practices to use when incorporating foreign currency accounting into the closing process. One is a highly regimented conversion process, so that exactly the same approach is used at the end of each reporting period. Doing so improves the efficiency of the close, and also reduces the risk of making mistakes. The other enhancement is making sure that there is a standard method for determining which exchange rates to use, and documenting them properly for later review by the auditors.

Summary

The translation of financial statements is a highly regimented process that requires great attention to the exchange rates used. It is also necessary to maintain exactly the same conversion template for all periods and all entities, to ensure that financial information is being rolled forward correctly from the subsidiaries. This is a much easier process when a company uses a company-wide financial reporting system, but if that is not the case, financial statement translation can represent a major bottleneck in the process of closing the books.

Chapter 2
Foreign Currency Transactions

Introduction

An organization engages in foreign currency transactions with business partners located in other countries. In these situations, it is likely that the entity will eventually have to hold foreign currencies or be paid with them. When it does so, the basic accounting for the transactions is relatively simple, and is noted in the following section. However, these transactions can also present the risk of exchange losses, which can be mitigated with the use of hedging transactions. In several following sections, we describe the nature of foreign exchange risk, the hedging concept, hedging instruments, and the accounting for hedges as they relate to foreign exchange situations.

Basic Foreign Currency Transactions

A business may enter into a transaction where it is scheduled to receive a payment from a customer that is denominated in a foreign currency, or to make a payment to a supplier in a foreign currency.

EXAMPLE

Micron Metallic enters into a transaction to pay £50,000 to a London-based manufacturer for a new stamping machine. Micron's functional currency is the U.S. dollar. Since Micron must pay in a foreign currency, this is considered a foreign currency transaction.

On the date of recognition of each such transaction, record it in the functional currency of the reporting entity, based on the exchange rate in effect on that date. This rule applies to the recordation of assets, liabilities, revenues, expenses, gains, and losses. If it is not possible to determine the market exchange rate on the date of recognition of a transaction, use the first exchange rate that is available on the next date on which foreign exchange transactions can be made.

If there is a change in the expected exchange rate between the functional currency of the entity and the currency in which a transaction is denominated, record a gain or loss in earnings in the period when the exchange rate changes; this is considered a foreign currency translation adjustment. This can result in the recognition of a series of gains or losses over a number of accounting periods, if the settlement date of a transaction is sufficiently far in the future. This also means that the stated balances of the related receivables and payables will reflect the current exchange rate as of each subsequent balance sheet date.

The two situations in which a gain or loss on a foreign currency transaction should not be recognized are:

- When a foreign currency transaction is designed to be an economic hedge of a net investment in a foreign entity, and is effective as such; or
- When there is no expectation of settling a transaction between entities that are to be consolidated. These transactions typically are of a long-term financing nature, such as advances or notes payable.

When a foreign currency transaction is settled, the related transaction gain or loss is included in the determination of net income.

EXAMPLE

Armadillo Industries sells goods to a company in the United Kingdom, to be paid in pounds having a value at the booking date of $100,000. Armadillo records this transaction with the following entry:

	Debit	Credit
Accounts receivable	100,000	
Sales		100,000

Later, when the customer pays Armadillo, the exchange rate has changed, resulting in a payment in pounds that translates to a $95,000 sale. Thus, the foreign exchange rate change related to the transaction has created a $5,000 loss for Armadillo, which it records with the following entry:

	Debit	Credit
Cash	95,000	
Foreign currency exchange loss	5,000	
Accounts receivable		100,000

Foreign Exchange Risk

When a business buys or sells across borders, it may need to use a foreign currency to settle these transactions. If so, the exchange rate between the entity's home currency and the foreign currency is continually changing. This means there is a risk that the company could be paid less by a customer than it is expecting, or be required to pay more to a supplier than it is expecting. An adverse change in an exchange rate could potentially wipe out the profit on a business deal.

There are several types of foreign exchange risk. A company may incur *transaction exposure*, which is derived from changes in foreign exchange rates between the dates when a transaction is booked and when it is settled. For example, a company in the United States may sell goods to a company in the United Kingdom, to be paid in pounds having a value at the booking date of $100,000. Later, when the customer pays the company, the exchange rate has changed, resulting in a payment in pounds that translates to a $95,000 sale. Thus, the foreign exchange rate change related to a transaction has created a $5,000 loss for the seller. The following table shows the impact of transaction exposure on different scenarios.

Risk When Transactions Denominated in Foreign Currency

	Import Goods	Export Goods
Reporting currency weakens	Loss	Gain
Reporting currency strengthens	Gain	Loss

When a company has foreign subsidiaries, it denominates the recorded amount of their assets and liabilities in the currency of the country in which the subsidiaries generate and expend cash, which is their functional currency. When the company reports its consolidated results, it converts these valuations to the home currency of the parent company, which may suffer a loss if exchange rates have declined from the last time when the financial statements were consolidated. This type of risk is known as *translation exposure*.

EXAMPLE

Suture Corporation has a subsidiary located in England, which has its net assets denominated in pounds. The reporting currency of Suture is U.S. dollars. At year-end, when the parent company consolidates the financial statements of its subsidiaries, the U.S. dollar has depreciated in comparison to the pound, resulting in a decline in the value of the subsidiary's net assets.

The following table shows the impact of translation exposure on different scenarios.

Risk When Net Assets Denominated in Foreign Currency

	Assets	Liabilities
Reporting currency weakens	Gain	Loss
Reporting currency strengthens	Loss	Gain

The Hedging Concept

In an earlier section of this chapter, we noted a situation in which a foreign currency transaction is designed to hedge a net investment in a foreign entity, which results in a gain or loss on a foreign currency transaction not being recognized. In this situation, it is possible to create a net investment hedge that is equal to or less than the carrying amount of the net assets of the foreign operation. *Hedging* is a risk reduction technique, under which an entity uses a derivative or similar instrument to offset future changes in the fair value or cash flows of an asset or liability. The ideal outcome of a hedge is when the distribution of probable outcomes is reduced, so that the size of any potential loss is reduced.

The accounting for such a hedge is to recognize any gains or losses on the hedge in other comprehensive income, but only for that portion of the hedge that is effective. Any other gains or losses on the hedge are to be recorded directly in earnings. If the parent entity ever disposes of the foreign operations, shift the cumulative net amount of any gains or losses recognized in other comprehensive income as part of the hedging instrument into earnings.

Hedge effectiveness is the amount of the changes in the fair value or cash flows of a hedged item that are offset by changes in the fair value or cash flows of a hedging instrument. A highly effective hedging transaction is one in which the net effect of a pairing of a hedged item and a hedging instrument is close to zero.

Foreign Exchange Hedging Instruments

This section describes a number of methods for hedging foreign currency transactions. The first type of hedge, which is a loan denominated in a foreign currency, is designed to offset translation risk. The remaining hedges target the transaction risk related to the currency fluctuations associated with either specific or aggregated business transactions.

Loan Denominated in a Foreign Currency

When a company is at risk of recording a loss from the translation of assets and liabilities into its home currency, it can hedge the risk by obtaining a loan denominated in the functional currency in which the assets and liabilities are recorded. The effect of this hedge is to neutralize any loss on translation of the subsidiary's net assets with a gain on translation of the loan, or vice versa.

EXAMPLE

Suture Corporation has a subsidiary located in London, and which does business entirely within England. Accordingly, the subsidiary's net assets are denominated in pounds. The net assets of the subsidiary are currently recorded at £10 million. To hedge the translation risk associated with these assets, Suture acquires a £10 million loan from a bank in London.

One month later, a change in the dollar/pound exchange rate results in a translation loss of $15,000 on the translation of the subsidiary's net assets into U.S. dollars. This amount is exactly offset by the translation gain of $15,000 on the liability associated with the £10 million loan.

Tip: An ideal way to create an offsetting loan is to fund the purchase or expansion of a foreign subsidiary largely through the proceeds of a long-term loan obtained within the same country, so that the subsidiary's assets are approximately cancelled out by the amount of the loan.

There are two problems with this type of hedge. First, it can be difficult to obtain a loan in the country in which the net assets are located. Second, the company will incur an interest expense on a loan that it would not otherwise need, though the borrowed funds could be invested to offset the interest expense.

The Forward Contract

A forward contract is an agreement under which a business agrees to buy a certain amount of foreign currency on a specific future date, and at a predetermined exchange rate. Forward exchange rates can be obtained for twelve months into the future; quotes for major currency pairs can be obtained for as much as five to ten years in the future. The exchange rate is comprised of the following elements:

- The spot price of the currency
- The bank's transaction fee
- An adjustment (up or down) for the interest rate differential between the two currencies. In essence, the currency of the country having a lower interest rate will trade at a premium, while the currency of the country having a higher interest rate will trade at a discount. For example, if the domestic interest rate is lower than the rate in the other country, the bank acting as the counterparty adds points to the spot rate, which increases the cost of the foreign currency in the forward contract.

The calculation of the number of discount or premium points to subtract from or add to a forward contract is based on the following formula:

$$\text{Exchange rate} \quad \times \quad \text{Interest rate differential} \quad \times \quad \frac{\text{Days in contract}}{360} \quad = \quad \text{Premium or discount}$$

Thus, if the spot price of pounds per dollar were 1.5459 and there were a premium of 15 points for a forward contract with a 360-day maturity, the forward rate (not including a transaction fee) would be 1.5474.

By entering into a forward contract, a company can ensure that a definite future liability can be settled at a specific exchange rate. Forward contracts are typically customized, and arranged between a company and its bank. The bank will require a partial payment to initiate a forward contract, as well as final payment shortly before the settlement date.

EXAMPLE

Suture Corporation has acquired computer software from a company in the United Kingdom, which Suture must pay for in 90 days in the amount of £220,000. To hedge against the risk of an unfavorable change in exchange rates during the intervening 90 days, Suture enters into a forward contract with its bank to buy £220,000 in 90 days, at the current exchange rate.

90 days later, the exchange rate has indeed taken a turn for the worse, but Suture's treasurer is indifferent, since he obtains the £220,000 needed for the purchase transaction based on the exchange rate in existence when the contract with the supplier was originally signed.

A forward contract is designed to have a specific settlement date, but the business transaction to which it relates may not be so timely. For example, a business has a contract to sell £10,000 in 60 days, but may not be able to do so if it has not yet received funds from a customer. A *forward window contract* is designed to work around this variability in the timing of receipts from customers by incorporating a range of settlement dates. One can then wait for a cash receipt and trigger settlement of the forward contract immediately thereafter.

The primary difficulties with forward contracts relate to their being customized transactions that are designed specifically for two parties. Because of this level of customization, it is difficult for either party to offload the contract to a third party. Also, the level of customization makes it difficult to compare offerings from different banks, so there is a tendency for banks to build unusually large fees into these contracts. Finally, a company may find that the underlying transaction for which a forward contract was created has been cancelled, leaving the contract still to be settled. If so, one can enter into a second forward contract, whose net effect is to offset the first forward contract. Though the bank will charge fees for both contracts, this arrangement will settle the company's obligations.

The Futures Contract

A futures contract is similar in concept to a forward contract, in that a business can enter into a contract to buy or sell currency at a specific price on a future date. The difference is that futures contracts are traded on an exchange, so these contracts are for standard amounts and durations. An initial deposit into a margin account is required to initiate a futures contract. The contract is then repriced each day, and if cumulative losses drain the margin account, a company is required to add more funds to the margin account. If the company does not respond to a margin call, the exchange closes out the contract.

Given that futures contracts are standardized, they may not exactly match the timing and amounts of an underlying transaction that is being hedged, which can lead to over- or under-hedging. However, since these contracts are traded on an exchange, it is easier to trade them than forward contracts, which allows one to easily unwind a hedge position earlier than its normal settlement date.

The Currency Option

An option gives its owner the right, but not the obligation, to buy or sell an asset at a certain price (known as the *strike price*), either on or before a specific date. In exchange for this right, the buyer pays an up-front premium to the seller. The income earned by the seller is restricted to the premium payment received, while the buyer has a theoretically unlimited profit potential, depending upon the future direction of the relevant exchange rate.

Currency options are available for the purchase or sale of currencies within a certain future date range, with the following variations available for the option contract:

- *American option.* The option can be exercised on any date within the option period, so that delivery is two business days after the exercise date.
- *European option.* The option can only be exercised on the expiry date, which means that delivery will be two business days after the expiry date.
- *Burmudan option.* The option can only be exercised on certain predetermined dates.

The holder of an option will exercise it when the strike price is more favorable than the current market rate, which is called being *in-the-money*. If the strike price is less favorable than the current market rate, this is called being *out-of-the-money*, in which case the option holder will not exercise the option. If the option holder is inattentive, it is possible that an in-the-money option will not be exercised prior to its expiry date. Notice of option exercise must be given to the counterparty by the notification date stated in the option contract.

A currency option provides two key benefits:

- *Loss prevention.* An option can be exercised to hedge the risk of loss, while still leaving open the possibility of benefiting from a favorable change in exchange rates.
- *Date variability.* One can exercise an option within a predetermined date range, which is useful when there is uncertainty about the exact timing of the underlying exposure.

There are a number of factors that enter into the price of a currency option, which can make it difficult to ascertain whether a quoted option price is reasonable. These factors are:

- The difference between the designated strike price and the current spot price. The buyer of an option can choose a strike price that suits his specific circumstances. A strike price that is well away from the current spot price will cost less, since the likelihood of exercising the option is low. However, setting such a strike price means that the buyer is willing to absorb the loss associated with a significant change in the exchange rate before seeking cover behind an option.
- The current interest rates for the two currencies during the option period.

- The duration of the option.
- The volatility of the market. This is the expected amount by which the currency is expected to fluctuate during the option period, with higher volatility making it more likely that an option will be exercised. Volatility is a guesstimate, since there is no quantifiable way to predict it.
- The willingness of counterparties to issue options.

Banks generally allow an option exercise period of no more than three months. Multiple partial currency deliveries within a currency option can be arranged.

Exchange traded options for standard quantities are available. This type of option eliminates the risk of counterparty failure, since the clearing house operating the exchange guarantees the performance of all options traded on the exchange.

EXAMPLE

Suture Corporation has an obligation to buy £250,000 in three months. Currently, the forward rate for the British pound is 1.5000 U.S. dollars, so that it should require $375,000 to buy the £250,000 in 90 days. If the pound depreciates, Suture will be able to buy pounds for less than the $375,000 that it currently anticipates spending, but if the pound appreciates, Suture will have to spend more to acquire the £250,000.

Suture's treasurer elects to buy an option, so that he can hedge against the appreciation of the pound, while leaving open the prospect of profits to be gained from any depreciation in the pound. The cost of an option with a strike price of 1.6000 U.S. dollars per pound is $3,000.

Three months later, the pound has appreciated against the dollar, with the price having changed to 1.75 U.S. dollars per pound. The treasurer exercises the option, and spends $400,000 for the requisite number of pounds (calculated as £250,000 × 1.6000). If he had not purchased the option, the purchase would instead have cost $437,500 (calculated as £250,000 × 1.7500). Thus, Suture saved $34,500 by using a currency option (calculated as the savings of $37,500, less the $3,000 cost of the option).

Currency options are particularly valuable during periods of high currency price volatility. Unfortunately from the perspective of the buyer, high volatility equates to higher option prices, since there is a higher probability that the counterparty will have to make a payment to the option buyer.

The Cylinder Option

Two options can be combined to create a *cylinder option*. One option is priced above the current spot price of the target currency, while the other option is priced below the spot price. The gain from exercising one option is used to partially offset the cost of the other option, thereby reducing the overall cost of the hedge. In effect, the upside potential offered by one option is being sold for a premium payment in order to finance the protection afforded by the opposing option.

The cylinder option is configured so that a company can acquire the right to buy currency at a specified price (a call option) and sell an option to a counterparty to buy currency from the company at a specified price (a put option), usually as of the expiry date. The premium the company pays for the purchased call is partially offset by the premium payable to the company for the put option that it sold.

If the market exchange rate remains between the boundaries established by the two currency options, the company never uses its options and instead buys or sells currency on the open market to fulfill its currency needs. If the market price breaches the strike price of the call option, the company exercises the call option and buys currency at the designated strike price. Conversely, if the market price breaches the strike price of the put option, the counterparty exercises its option to sell the currency to the company.

A variation on the cylinder option is to construct call and put options that are very close together, so that the premium cost of the call is very close to the premium income generated by the put, resulting in a near-zero net hedging cost to the company. The two options have to be very close together for the zero cost option to work, which means that the effective currency price range being hedged is quite small.

Swaps

If a company has or expects to have an obligation to make a payment in a foreign currency, it can arrange to swap currency holdings with a third party that already has the required currency. The two entities engage in a swap transaction by agreeing upon an initial swap date, the date when the cash positions will be reversed back to their original positions, and an interest rate that reflects the comparative differences in interest rates between the two countries in which the entities are located.

Another use for a currency swap is when a forward exchange contract has been delayed. In this situation, one would normally sell to a counterparty the currency that it has just obtained through the receipt of an account receivable. If, however, the receivable has not yet been paid, the company can enter into a swap agreement to obtain the required currency and meet its immediate obligation under the forward exchange contract. Later, when the receivable is eventually paid, the company can reverse the swap, returning funds to the counterparty.

A swap arrangement may be for just a one-day period, or extend out for several years into the future. Swap transactions generally do not occur in amounts of less than $5 million, so this technique is not available to smaller businesses.

A potentially serious problem with swaps is the prospect of a default by the counterparty. If there is a default, the company once again assumes its foreign currency liability, and must now scramble to find an alternative hedge.

Hedge Accounting - General

The accounting for hedges involves matching a derivative instrument to a hedged item, and then recognizing gains and losses from both items in the same period. A derivative is always measured at its fair value. If the instrument is effective for a period of time, this may mean that incremental changes in its fair value are continually being recorded in the accounting records.

The intent behind hedge accounting is to allow a business to record changes in the value of a hedging relationship in other comprehensive income, rather than in earnings. This is done in order to protect the core earnings of a business from periodic variations in the value of its financial instruments before they have been liquidated. Once a financial instrument has been liquidated, any accumulated gains or losses stored in other comprehensive income are shifted into earnings.

When a business uses a derivative as a hedge, it can elect to designate the derivative as belonging to one of the following hedging classifications:

- *Cash flow hedge.* The derivative is used to hedge variations in the cash flows associated with an asset or liability, or of a forecasted transaction.
- *Foreign currency hedge.* The derivative is used to hedge variations in the foreign currency exposure associated with a net investment in a foreign operation, a forecasted transaction, an available-for-sale security, or an unrecognized firm commitment.

If a derivative instrument is designated as belonging within one of these classifications, the gains or losses associated with the hedge are matched to any gains or losses incurred by the asset or liability with which the derivative is paired. However, the hedging relationship must first qualify for hedge accounting. To do so, the relationship must meet all of the following criteria:

- *Designation.* The hedging relationship must be designated as such at its inception. The documentation of the relationship must include the following:
    - The hedging relationship
    - The risk management objective and strategy, which includes identification of the hedging instrument and the hedged item, the nature of the risk being hedged, and the method used to determine hedge effectiveness and ineffectiveness.
    - If there is a cash flow hedge of a forecasted transaction, the period when the forecasted transaction will occur, the nature of the asset or liability involved, either the amount of foreign exchange being hedged or the number of items encompassed by the transaction, and the current price of the forecasted transaction.
- *Eligibility (hedged item).* Only certain types of assets and liabilities can qualify for special accounting as a hedging relationship.
- *Eligibility (hedging item).* Designate either all or a portion of the hedging instrument as such. Also, several derivative instruments can be jointly designated as the hedging instrument.
- *Effectiveness.* There is an expectation that the pairing will result in a highly effective hedge that offsets prospective changes in the fair values or cash flows associated with the hedged risk. A highly effective hedge is one in which the change in fair values or cash flows of the hedge falls between 80%

and 125% of the opposing change in the fair values or cash flows of the financial instrument that is being hedged. A regression analysis can be used instead of these percentage boundaries to determine hedge effectiveness. Over the life of a hedging relationship, the effectiveness of the pairing must be examined at least quarterly. A prospective analysis should also be made to estimate whether the relationship will be highly effective in future periods, typically using a probability-weighted analysis of changes in fair values or cash flows. If the relationship is no longer highly effective through the date of this assessment, then the pairing no longer qualifies for hedge accounting.

Even if a hedge is considered to be effective, it is quite possible that some portion of the risk inherent in an underlying transaction will not be covered by a hedge. In this situation, gains and losses on the unhedged portion of a hedged pairing should be recorded in earnings.

EXAMPLE

Suture Corporation pays $1 million for an investment that is denominated in pounds. Suture's treasurer enters into a hedging transaction that is also denominated in pounds, and which is designed to be a hedge of the investment. One year later, Suture experiences a loss of $12,000 on the investment and a $9,000 gain on the hedging instrument. The full $9,000 gain on the hedging instrument is considered effective, so only the difference between the investment and its hedge - $3,000 – is recorded as a loss in earnings.

There may be cases in which a hedging instrument is being employed, where the third party is actually another entity under the umbrella of a parent company. In this case, risk is not being offloaded to a third party. Consequently, such a hedging instrument is not considered to be a hedge for the purposes of hedge accounting.

Hedge Accounting – Cash Flow Hedges

There could be variations in the cash flows associated with an asset or liability or a forecasted transaction, which may affect the profits of a business. A cash flow hedge is designed to hedge against this exposure to changes in cash flows that are caused by a specific risk. It is possible to only hedge the risks associated with a portion of an asset, liability, or forecasted transaction, as long as the effectiveness of the related hedge can be measured. The accounting for a cash flow hedge is as follows:

- *Hedging item.* Recognize the effective portion of any gain or loss in other comprehensive income, and recognize the ineffective portion of any gain or loss in earnings.
- *Hedged item.* Initially recognize the effective portion of any gain or loss in other comprehensive income. Reclassify these gains or losses into earnings when the forecasted transaction affects earnings.

There are several additional special situations involving cash flow hedges that require different accounting transactions. The following scenarios reveal the more likely accounting variations:

1. *Exclusions from strategy.* If the documented risk management strategy does not include a certain component of the gains or losses experienced by the hedged item, recognize this excluded amount in earnings. Doing so reduces the aggregate amount of gains or losses in other comprehensive income. Next;

2. *Adjust other comprehensive income.* Reduce the amount of accumulated other comprehensive income related to a hedging relationship to the lesser of:

    - The cumulative gain or loss on the derivative from the date when the hedge began, less any gains or losses already reclassified into earnings; or
    - The cumulative gain or loss on the derivative that will be needed to offset the cumulative change in expected future cash flows on the hedged transaction from the date when the hedge began, less any gains or losses already reclassified into earnings.

3. *Further gain or loss recognition.* Recognize in earnings any remaining gain or loss on the hedging derivative, or to revise the accumulated other comprehensive income amount to match the balance derived in step 2.

4. *Foreign currency adjustments.* If a foreign currency position is being hedged, and hedge effectiveness is based on the total changes in the cash flow of an option, then reclassify from other comprehensive income to earnings an amount sufficient to adjust earnings for the amortization of the option cost.

A key issue with cash flow hedges is when to recognize gains or losses in earnings when the hedging transaction relates to a forecasted transaction. These gains or losses should be reclassified from other comprehensive income to earnings when the hedged transaction affects earnings.

EXAMPLE

Suture Corporation has acquired equipment from a company in the United Kingdom, which Suture must pay for in 60 days in the amount of £150,000. Suture's functional currency is the U.S. Dollar. At the time of the purchase, Suture could settle this obligation for $240,000, based on the exchange rate then in effect.

To hedge against the risk of an unfavorable change in exchange rates during the intervening 60 days, Suture enters into a forward contract with its bank to buy £150,000 in 60 days, at the current exchange rate. Suture's controller designates the forward contract as a hedge of its exposure to adverse changes in the dollar to pounds exchange rate.

At the end of the next month, the pound has increased in value against the dollar, so that it would now require $242,000 to settle the obligation. Luckily, the value of the forward contract has also increased by $2,000, which results in the following entry:

	Debit	Credit
Forward asset (asset)	2,000	
Other comprehensive income		2,000

The exchange rate remains the same for the following month, after which the treasurer settles the forward contract and the controller records the following entry:

	Debit	Credit
Cash (asset)	2,000	
Forward asset (asset)		2,000

The payables staff then pays the $242,000 obligation to the United Kingdom supplier, as noted in the following entry. The transaction also includes a $2,000 reduction of the purchase price, which represents the deferred gain on the forward contract.

	Debit	Credit
Fixed assets – Equipment (asset)	240,000	
Other comprehensive income	2,000	
Cash (asset)		242,000

The net result of this hedging transaction is that Suture has used a hedging instrument to offset the risk of an adverse change in the applicable exchange rate, and so is able to pay for the equipment at the original purchase price.

Cash flow hedge accounting should be terminated at once if any of the following situations arise:

- The hedging arrangement is no longer effective
- The hedging instrument expires or is terminated
- The organization revokes the hedging designation

If it is probable that the hedged forecasted transaction will not occur within the originally-stated time period or within two months after this period, shift the derivative's gain or loss from accumulated other comprehensive income to earnings.

Hedge Accounting – Net Investment Hedges

A business may have an investment in operations in another country. If so, changes in the exchange rate between the functional currency of the parent entity and the currency of the foreign operations could create gains or losses. In this situation, it is possible to create a net investment hedge that is equal to or less than the carrying amount of the net assets of the foreign operation.

The accounting for such a hedge is to recognize any gains or losses on the hedge in other comprehensive income, but only for that portion of the hedge that is effective. Any other gains or losses on the hedge are to be recorded directly into earnings. If the parent entity ever disposes of the foreign operations, shift the cumulative net amount of any gains or losses recognized in other comprehensive income as part of the hedging instrument into earnings.

EXAMPLE

Suture Corporation invests $20 million in a new subsidiary located in England. The functional currency of this subsidiary is the pound. The exchange rate on the investment date is $1 = £0.6463, so the initial investment is priced at £12,926,000. Suture takes out a loan in England in the amount of £9,695,000 (which translates to $15,000,000) and designates it as a hedge of its investment in the subsidiary. The stated strategy is that any change in the fair value of the loan attributed to foreign exchange risk will offset 75% of the translation gains or losses on the Suture investment.

One year later, the exchange rate has changed to $1 = £0.6600, which yields the following loss on the investment for Suture:

$$(£12,926,000 \div 0.6600 = \$19,585,000) - \$20,000,000$$

$$= -\$415,000 \text{ Investment translation loss}$$

Against this loss is set the following gain on the related loan:

$$(£9,695,000 \div 0.6600 = \$14,689,000) - \$15,000,000$$

$$= \$311,000 \text{ Loan translation gain}$$

Suture creates the following entry to record the reduction in value of its investment, as well as the translation gain related to its loan:

	Debit	Credit
Cumulative translation adjustment	415,000	
Investment in subsidiary		415,000
Pound-denominated debt	311,000	
Cumulative translation adjustment		311,000

Unhedged Foreign Exchange Gains and Losses

There may be circumstances when a choice is made not to create a hedge against a foreign exchange position, and the company subsequently incurs a gain or loss on that position. It is also possible that the company does not have an adequate foreign exchange forecasting system, and so does not know that it even has unhedged positions, which will most certainly result in unhedged gains or losses.

In either case, it is extremely useful to keep track of gains or losses arising from unhedged foreign currency positions, in order to estimate when the size of these gains or losses warrants the imposition of a more extensive hedging program. The simplest form of metric is a trend line analysis. This trend line will likely yield results that routinely bounce between gains and losses. The key issue to watch for is an increasing trend in the *size* of the gains or losses over time. When they become large enough to seriously impact the company's reported results from operations, it is time to consider a combination of a better forecasting system and a more active hedging program.

Inclusion in Impairment Analysis

A business may have an investment in a foreign entity. If so, and as noted earlier, it may have created a hedge against the risk of a translation loss in its investment in the foreign entity. If so, there may be gains or losses associated with the hedge that are listed in other comprehensive income; these gains or losses should be considered when conducting a periodic review of the foreign entity to see if the investment has been impaired. For example, a gain on an investment hedge increases the carrying amount of the investment for impairment testing purposes, while a loss an investment hedge would reduce the carrying amount.

Summary

The accounting for derivatives and hedges is among the most complex in all of accounting, especially for outlier situations where the circumstances must be closely examined to ensure that the proper accounting rules are followed. In many instances, and especially when the accountant is dealing with a new transaction, it can make sense to consult with the company's auditors regarding the proper accounting to use.

The payoff for this high level of accounting complexity is a delay in the recognition of gains or losses in earnings. If management is not concerned about more immediate recognition, or if the gains or losses are minor, it may make sense to ignore the multitude of compliance issues associated with hedge accounting. Instead, simply create hedges as needed and record gains or losses on foreign exchange holdings and hedges at once, without worrying about the proper documentation of each hedging relationship and having to repeatedly measure hedge effectiveness.

Chapter 3
Other Foreign Currency Topics

Introduction

When rating the risk of incorrect reporting for different accounting transactions, activities related to foreign currencies can score fairly high, because there are so many steps involved in translating the transactions correctly. There is also a high risk of using the wrong exchange rates. Given these concerns, we have noted in the following section a list of internal audit tasks that can be used to identify issues related to foreign currencies.

There are not an excessive number of disclosures specifically pertaining to foreign currency transactions. Those required by GAAP are noted later in this chapter, along with relevant examples.

Internal Audit Tasks

The internal audit staff should review certain aspects of foreign currency accounting at regular intervals. The intent is to ensure that the correct exchange rates are being used for translation calculations, as well as to verify that the translation calculations are correct. At a minimum, these reviews are needed prior to year-end, when the outside auditors will assuredly examine these items. More specifically, here are several internal audit tasks to complete:

- *Exchange rate verification.* If the currency of an entity must first be translated into the functional currency, or when the financial statements are being translated into the reporting currency, verify that the historical exchange rates used were correct, and were applied to the correct balance sheet line items. If average exchange rates were used, verify their calculation.
- *Calculation verification.* Verify that all calculations used to translate the financial statements to the reporting currency are correct (this is more of an issue if an electronic spreadsheet is used).
- *Verify LCM adjustments.* In the rare case where the currency used by a business is not its functional currency, verify that lower of cost or market adjustments have been made, and check the accuracy of these adjustments.
- *Verify noncontrolling interests allocation.* If there are noncontrolling interests, verify that the amount of any accumulated translation adjustment allocated to these interests is correct.
- *Hyperinflationary treatment.* If an entity is located in what is considered to be a hyperinflationary environment, verify the accuracy of the initial designation, as well as the argument later used to stop hyperinflationary economy treatment. Further, at the end of the designated hyperinflationary period, verify that the conversion back to the use of the local currency is correct.

- *Monitor AOCI.* Routinely review the amount of transaction adjustment gains and losses located in accumulated other comprehensive income (AOCI) to see if any of these amounts should be recognized in earnings.
- *Verify hedge documentation.* Review all significant hedge transactions to verify that they have been properly documented, and that the designated hedges are effective.

If there have been recurring instances in which the internal audit staff has found issues with the accounting for foreign exchange transactions, schedule more frequent reviews of the problem areas.

Foreign Currency Disclosures

Any accounting policies related to foreign currency translation can be stated in the accounting policies section of the financial statement disclosures. Sample policies are:

> The company's worldwide operations utilize the U.S. dollar or local currency as the functional currency, where applicable. For subsidiaries where the U.S. dollar (USD) is the functional currency, all foreign currency asset and liability amounts are remeasured into USD at end-of-period exchange rates, except for inventories, prepaid expenses, property, plant and equipment, goodwill and other intangible assets, which are remeasured at historical rates. Foreign currency income and expenses are remeasured at average exchange rates in effect during the year, except for expenses related to balance sheet amounts remeasured at historical exchange rates. Exchange gains and losses arising from remeasurement of foreign currency-denominated monetary assets and liabilities are included in income in the period in which they occur.

> For subsidiaries where the local currency is the functional currency, assets and liabilities denominated in local currencies are translated into USD at end-of-period exchange rates and the resultant translation adjustments are reported, net of their related tax effects, as a component of accumulated other comprehensive income (loss) in equity. Assets and liabilities denominated in other than the local currency are remeasured into the local currency prior to translation into USD and the resultant exchange gains or losses are included in income in the period in which they occur. Income and expenses are translated into USD at average exchange rates in effect during the period.

Disclose the following information related to transactions denominated in foreign currencies:

- *Gains and losses.* If there are transaction-based gains or losses during the period that are caused by changes in foreign exchange rates, disclose the aggregate amount in the financial statements or in the accompanying notes. For example:

> Net currency transaction gains and losses included in other (income) expense were losses of $10 million, $8 million and $7 million in 20X3, 20X2 and 20X1, respectively.

- *Subsequent rate changes*. If there is a foreign currency rate change after the date of the financial statements that has a significant effect on unsettled balances, disclose the impact of the rate on unsettled transactions between the date of the financial statements and the date of the rate change. If it is not possible to determine these changes, state that fact.
- *Rate change effects*. GAAP encourages a reporting entity to discuss the effects of rate changes on the results of its operations, but does not require it. This discussion might include the effects of rate changes on selling prices, sales volume, and the cost structure of the business. For example:

> Our revenue and operating income are subject to variability due to the effects of foreign currency fluctuations against the U.S. dollar. We have exposure to approximately 30 functional currencies. We endeavor to mitigate the effects of currency fluctuations by our hedging strategy; however, certain significant currency fluctuations could adversely affect our results of operations, including sales and gross margins.

If translation adjustments have been reported in equity, disclose an analysis of the changes during the period in the financial statements. This information can be integrated into the statement of changes in equity, or stated separately in the accompanying disclosures, or in a separate financial statement. The analysis should include the information in the following table.

Equity Adjustment from Foreign Currency Translation

	Beginning balance of cumulative translation adjustments
+/-	The aggregate adjustment caused by translation adjustments, as well as from the gains and losses caused by certain hedges and intra-entity balances
+/-	The amount of income taxes allocated to translation adjustments
+/-	Transfers from cumulative translation adjustments as a result of the sale or liquidation of an investment in a foreign entity
=	Ending balance of cumulative translation adjustments

If there are income taxes associated with translation adjustments, report them in other comprehensive income.

If a company is publicly-held, Item 7A of the annual Form 10-K contains a requirement pertaining to the reporting of risks related to exchange rates. The essential reporting requirements for exchange rate risks are as follows (with foreign currency references noted in bold):

- Provide quantitative information about market risk as of the end of the latest fiscal year, subdividing information by instruments entered into for trading purposes and instruments entered into for purposes other than trading. Within these categories, present information for each market risk exposure category, such as for interest rate risk, **foreign currency exchange rate risk,** commodity price risk, and other relevant market risks. This information may be presented using any one of the following three disclosure alternatives:

- A tabular presentation, from which a reader can determine future cash flows.
- A sensitivity analysis that discloses the potential loss in future earnings, fair values, or cash flows based on hypothetical changes in interest rates, **foreign currency exchange rates**, commodity prices, and so forth over time.
- A value at risk disclosure that expresses the potential loss in future earnings, fair values, or cash flows of market risk sensitive instruments over a period of time, with a likelihood of occurrence, from changes in interest rates, **foreign currency exchange rates**, commodity prices, and other relevant market rates or prices. For each category for which value at risk disclosures are made, provide either:
  - The average, high and low amounts, or the distribution of the value at risk amounts for the reporting period; or
  - The average, high and low amounts, or the distribution of actual changes in fair values, earnings, or cash flows from the market risk sensitive instruments occurring during the reporting period; or
  - The percentage or number of times the actual changes in fair values, earnings, or cash flows from the market risk sensitive instruments exceeded the value at risk amounts during the reporting period

- Describe the company's primary market exposures, how these exposures are managed (noting objectives, strategies, and any instruments used), and changes in the company's primary market risk exposures.

For example:

In the normal course of business and consistent with established policies and procedures, we employ a variety of financial instruments to manage exposure to fluctuations in the value of foreign currencies. It is our policy to utilize these financial instruments only where necessary to finance our business and manage such exposures; we do not enter into these transactions for trading or speculative purposes.

We are exposed to foreign currency fluctuations, primarily as a result of our international sales, product sourcing and funding activities. Our foreign exchange risk management program is intended to lessen both the positive and negative effects of currency fluctuations on our consolidated results of operations, financial position and cash flows. We use forward exchange contracts and options to hedge certain anticipated but not yet firmly committed transactions as well as certain firm commitments and the related receivables and payables, including third-party and intercompany transactions. We have, and may in the future, also use forward contracts to hedge our investment in the net assets of certain international subsidiaries to offset foreign currency translation adjustments related to our net investment in those subsidiaries. Where exposures are hedged, our program has the effect of delaying the impact of exchange rate movements on our consolidated financial statements.

The timing for hedging exposures, as well as the type and duration of the hedge instruments employed, are guided by our hedging policies and determined based upon the nature of the exposure and prevailing market conditions. Generally, hedged transactions are expected to be recognized within 12 to 18 months. Hedged transactions are principally denominated in Euros, British Pounds and Japanese Yen.

We monitor foreign exchange risk and related derivatives using a variety of techniques including a review of market value, sensitivity analysis, and value-at-risk (VaR). Our market-sensitive derivative and other financial instruments are foreign currency forward contracts and foreign currency option contracts.

We use VaR to monitor the foreign exchange risk of our foreign currency forward and foreign currency option derivative instruments only. The VaR determines the maximum potential one-day loss in the fair value of these foreign exchange rate-sensitive financial instruments. The VaR model estimates assume normal market conditions and a 95% confidence level. There are various modeling techniques that can be used in the VaR computation. Our computations are based on interrelationships between currencies and interest rates. These interrelationships are a function of foreign exchange currency market changes and interest rate changes over the preceding one year period. The value of foreign currency options does not change on a one-to-one basis with changes in the underlying currency rate.

The VaR model is a risk analysis tool and does not purport to represent actual losses in fair value that we will incur, nor does it consider the potential effect of favorable changes in market rates. It also does not represent the full extent of the possible loss that may occur. Actual future gains and losses will differ from those estimated because of changes or differences in market rates and interrelationships, hedging instruments and hedge percentages, timing and other factors.

The estimated maximum one-day loss in fair value on our foreign currency sensitive derivative financial instruments, derived using the VaR model, was $0.9 million and $0.5 million at December 31, 20X3 and 20X2, respectively. The VaR increased year-over-year as a result of an increase in the total notional value of our foreign currency derivative portfolio combined with a longer average duration on our outstanding trades at December 31, 20X3. Such a hypothetical loss in the fair value of our derivatives would be offset by increases in the value of the underlying transactions being hedged.

Summary

An initial examination of the internal audit tasks noted in this chapter may uncover specific areas in which there are variances from expectations, while other areas are quite clean. These findings will point toward the imposition of new controls, procedures, and training, after which it will be necessary to follow up with additional reviews to determine whether the changes have improved the results of the system.

In the preceding section, we described only those disclosures specifically pertaining to foreign currency issues. There are more disclosures relating to hedging activities, which are described in the author's *Accounting for Derivatives and Hedges* book.

Glossary

D

Derivative financial instrument. A financial contract whose value depends on the price of an underlying asset or benchmark.

E

Exchange rate. The ratio at which a unit of one currency can be exchanged for another currency.

F

Foreign currency. A currency other than the functional currency being used by an entity.

Foreign currency transactions. Any transactions having terms that are denominated in a currency other than the functional currency used by a reporting entity.

Foreign currency translation. The process of converting amounts stated in a foreign currency into the reporting currency of the parent entity.

Foreign entity. An entity whose financial statements use a currency other than the reporting currency of its parent, and whose results are combined with those of a parent entity.

Foreign exchange risk. The risk that the value of an investment will be reduced by changes in the applicable foreign exchange rate.

Functional currency. The currency that an entity uses in the majority of its business transactions.

Futures contract. A standardized agreement to buy or sell a financial instrument at a specific price and on a specific date, which can be traded on an exchange.

G

GAAP. An acronym for Generally Accepted Accounting Principles.

H

Hedge. An action taken to reduce an existing or expected risk.

L

Local currency. The legal currency being used within a country.

N

Noncontrolling interest. That portion of the equity in a subsidiary that is not attributable to the parent entity.

O

Option. A contract that gives the holder the right, but not the obligation, to purchase or sell an asset at a specific price for a designated period of time.

R

Reporting currency. The currency in which a business prepares its financial statements.

Reporting entity. The organization issuing financial statements.

S

Spot price. The price at which a currency can currently be purchased.

Strike price. The price at which an option or other similar contract can be exercised.

T

Transaction date. The date on which a business transaction is recorded in the accounting records of an organization.

Transaction gain or loss. A gain or loss resulting from a change in the exchange rate between the functional currency of an entity and the currency in which the transaction was denominated.

Translation adjustments. Corrections arising from the translation of financial statements from a functional currency to the reporting currency.

Index